Reading Your Way Around Japan

Reading Your Way Around Japan

By
Boye De Mente

LOTUS PRESS LIMITED
Tokyo, Japan

PHOENIX BOOKS
Arizona, U.S.A.

Published By Lotus Press Limited
Chofu P.O. Box 15, Tokyo 182–91, Japan
Copyright © in Japan 1978 by Boye De Mente
All rights reserved

Distributor in U.S.A.
Phoenix Books/Publishers
1641 E. McClellan Blvd,
Phoenix, Arizona 85016

Cover by Akira Tsuchiya
Printed By Komiyama Printing Co.
Manufactured in Japan
ISBN 0–914778–20–X

Contents

Getting the Signs Right!

Being able to read signs is probably more important in Japan than in any other country. There are signs everywhere, many of them of vital importance to visitors and residents alike.

While there are some English-language signs in Tokyo and along Japan's "Tourist Trail," most of the signs—even in cosmopolitan cities—are in *kanji* characters.

The average non-Japanese reading visitor in Japan is therefore constantly "in the dark" to some degree, and often seriously inconvenienced by not knowing that 会計 means "Cashier," that 南口 means "South Exit" or that 駐車禁止 means "No Parking."

This little booklet is designed to take some of the mystery and inconvenience out of your visit to Tokyo and Japan. It includes some 200 of the Japanese-language signs you are most likely to "meet" and need to know during your visit.

Remember that each *kanji* symbol is pronounced the same as its romanized spelling, which is also given in phonetics to help you pronounce the signs.

How to Pronounce Japanese

This handbook is designed to serve as a pocketguide for English-reading travelers who have had absolutely no experience with the Japanese language. It can be used immediately without prior preparation or study if the traveler so desires.

The Japanese language is based on only six key sounds. These six sounds are the basis for an "alphabet" of some 100 syllables. Originally these syllables were written only in *Japanese*, (that is, not in the Roman alphabet that we use). But one of the first American missionaries to Japan, Dr. Charles Hepburn, worked out a system of spelling Japanese with the familiar ABC's.

This system of spelling out Japanese words, called *Romaji* (phonetically: roe-mah-jee) by the Japanese, makes it possible to study or read the language without having to learn the tremendously complicated Chinese ideographs with which it has traditionally been written.

A foreigner who has never heard Japanese spoken can learn how to pronounce it correctly in just a few minutes. Students and others who claim that the language is difficult to pronounce are mistaken. They confuse the difficulty of getting several words out in a smooth flow with pronunciation, which is simply making the sounds of individual words.

By following very simple directions explained below you can teach yourself to properly pronounce Japanese in the next ten minutes. This will allow you to memorize the few key sentences needed to make your trip to Japan much more rewarding.

Since many travelers don't have the time (or patience) to accomplish this small chore, however, every Japanese word or phrase in the guide is also spelled out phonetically. All you have to do, if you don't want to take the time to memorize the pronounciation of the *Romaji* spelling, is read the phonetically spelled version as if it actually were English.

All except one of the 100 or so syllables in the Japanese alphabet are based on the five Romanized vowel sounds: A, I, U, E, O (pronounced Ah, Ee, Oou, Eh, Oh). The one exception is represented in our alphabet by the letter "N" and is pronounced like the "n" in the word "bond".

The syllables based on these sounds are:

1

		ka	**ki**	**ku**	**ke**	**ko**
Phonetically		(cah)	(key)	(coo)	(kay)	(coe)
		sa	**shi**	**su**	**se**	**so**
"	. . . . .	(sah)	(she)	(sue)	(say)	(so)
		ta	**chi**	**tsu**	**te**	**to**
"	. . . . .	(tah)	(chee)	(t'sue)	(tay)	(toe)
		na	**ni**	**nu**	**ne**	**no**
"	. . . . .	(nah)	(knee)	(new)	(nay)	(no)
		ha	**hi**	**hu**	**he**	**ho**
"	. . . . .	(ha!)	(he)	(who)	(hey)	(ho!)
		ma	**mi**	**mu**	**me**	**mo**
"	. . . . .	(mah)	(me)	(moo)	(may)	(moe)
		ya	**i**	**u**	**e**	**yo**
"	. . . . .	(yah)	(ee)	(oou)	(eh!)	(yoe)

	ra	**ri**	**ru**	**re**	**ro**
phonetically	(rah)	(ree)	(rue)	(ray)	(roe)

(trill the R's a bit it you can)

	wa				**wo**
"	(wah)				(oh)

	n
"	(like the "n" in bond)

2

	ga	**gi**	**gu**	**ge**	**go**
Phonetically	(gah)	(gee)	(goo)	(gay)	(go)
	za	**ji**	**zu**	**ze**	**zo**
"	(zah)	(jee)	(zoo)	(zay)	(zoe)
	da	**ji**	**zu**	**de**	**do**
"	(dah)	(jee)	(zoo)	(day)	(doe)
	ba	**bi**	**bu**	**be**	**bo**
"	(bah)	(bee)	(boo)	(bay)	(boe)
	pa	**pi**	**pu**	**pe**	**po**
"	(pah)	(pee)	(poo)	(pay)	(poe)

The following 33 syllables are combinations of some of those appearing in the two sets above. Their pronounciation follows exactly the same pattern.

	rya	**ryu**	**ryo**
Phonetically	(r'yah)	(r'you)	(r'roe)
	mya	**myu**	**myo**
''	(m'yah)	(m'you)	(m'yoe)
	nya	**nyu**	**nyo**
''	(n'yah)	(n'you)	(n'yoe)
	hya	**hyu**	**hyo**
''	(h'yah)	(h'you)	(h'yoe)
	cha	**chu**	**cho**
''	(chah)	(chew)	(choe)
	sha	**shu**	**sho**
''	(shah)	(shoe)	(show)
	kya	**kyu**	**kyo**
''	(q'yah)	(que)	(q'yoe)
	pya	**pyu**	**pyo**
''	(p'yah)	(p'you)	(p'yoe)
	bya	**byu**	**byo**
Phonetically	(b'yah)	(b'you)	(b'yoe)
	ja	**ju**	**jo**
''	(jah)	(jew)	(joe)
	gya	**gyu**	**gyo**
''	(g'yah)	(g'you)	(g'yoe)

If you want to use the Hepburn spelling (and not the Englishized phonetic spelling), it is important to look at the *Romaji* syllables closely and memorize their individual appearance and sound. For example the word *bengoshi* (lawyer) is made up of the four syllables be-n-go-shi (phonetically: bay-n-go-she). Pronounce it by syllables according to either the Hepburn system or phonetically and you can't miss.

On occasion the combination of two or more Japanese syllables forms the sound of some common English word. For example, the syllables "ko" and "n" 'kon), referring to a shade of blue, are pronounced like the English word "cone". In several instances I have used such words in preference to the strictly phonetic spelling.

Editor's Note

All of the *Kanji* (Khan-jee) or ideograms (characters) appearing in this book are set in Brush print-type, although the signs you will meet in Japan may be printed in one of several type styles—or hand-lettered in some unique style.

Most signs, however, will be in a Brush style called *Kyokasho-Tai,* a san serif type called *Gōchiku-Tai* or a serif style known as *Mincho-Tai.*

These three type styles are fairly similar, and should not cause you any recognition problems—as can be seen from the examples reproduced here:

A. Brush Type   — Kyokasho-Tai   中 央 線

B. San Serif   — Gochiku-Tai   中 央 線

C. Serif   — Mincho-Tai   中 央 線

The most important thing to keep in mind about Japanese writing is that the strokes must create a recognizable "picture" or symbol in order to have meaning. This of course limits the degree of stylization that may be used.

For your reference, the following character, which is read *Ei* (Aee) meaning eternal, contains all of the 8 strokes used in Japanese printing.

airport signs

Airline KOKU (Koe-Kuu)	航　　空 こうくう
Airline Ticket KOKU KEN (Koe-kuu ken)	航　空　券 こうくうけん
Airport KUKO (Kuu-koe)	空　　港 くうこう
All Nippon Airways ZENNIKU (Zen-nee-kuu)	全　日　空 ぜんにっくう
Arrival TOCHAKU (Toe-chah-kuu)	到　　着 とうちゃく

Boarding Pass TOJO KEN (Toe-joe-ken)	搭 乗 券 とうじょうけん
Bus BASU (Bah-sue)	バ ス ばす
Customs Office ZEIKAN (Zay-ee-khan)	税 関 ぜいかん
Departure SHUPPATSU (Shupe-pot-sue)	出 発 しゅっぱつ
Destination MOKUTEKICHI (Moe-kuu-tay-key-chee)	目 的 地 もくてきち

Domestic Lines KOKUNAI SEN (Koe-kuu-nie-sen)	国 内 線 こくないせん
Economy Class EKONOMI KURASU (A-koe-no-me kuu-rah-sue)	エコノミークラス えこのみーくらす
Fare UNCHIN (Uun-cheen)	運 賃 うんちん
First Class FASTO KURASU (Fahs-toe kuu-rah-sue)	ファーストクラス ふぁーすとくらす
Immigration SHUTSU NYUGOKU KANRI (Shoot-sue n'you-koe- kuu kahn-ree)	出入国管理 しゅつにゅうごくかんり

Information ANNAIGAKARI (Ahn-nie-gah-kah-ree)	案 内 係 あんないがかり
International Lines KOKUSAI SEN (Koke-sie sen)	国 際 線 こくさいせん
Japan Airlines NIHON KOKU (Nee hone koe-kuu)	日本航空 にほんこうくう
Monorail MONOREYRU (Moe-no-ray-e-rue)	モノレール ものれーる
Passport PASUPOTO (Pah-sue-poe-toe)	パスポート ぱすぽーと

Reservation YOYAKU (Yoe-yah-kuu)	予　　約 よやく
Tax-Free Shop MENZEI TEN (Mane-zay-e ten)	免　税　店 めんぜいてん
Taxi TAKUSHI (Tah-kuu-she)	タクシー たくしー
Transfer NORIKAE (No-ree-kie)	乗　換　え のりかえ
Visa SASHO (Sah-show)	査　　証 さしょう

bank signs

Bank GINKO (Gheen-koe)	銀　　行 ぎんこう
Cashier GENKIN SUITO (Gane-keen sue-e-toe)	現金出納 げんきんすいとう
Check KOGITTE (Koe-geet-tay)	小　切　手 こぎって
Deposit YOKIN (Yoe-keen)	預　　金 よきん
Exchange RYOGAE (Rio-guy)	両　替 りょうがえ

Foreign Exchange GAIKOKU KAWASE (Guy-koe-kuu kah-wah-say)	外国為替 がいこくかわせ
Ordinary Deposit FUTSU YOKIN (Fute-sue Yoe-keen)	普通預金 ふつうよきん
Paying SHIHARAI (She-hah-rye)	支 払 い しはらい
Remittance SOKIN (Soe-keen)	送　　　金 そうきん
Traveler's Checks RYOKO KOGITTE (Rio-koe koe-geet-tay)	旅行小切手 りょこうこぎって

Daiichi Kangyo Bank DAIICHI KANGYO GINKO (Die-e-chee khan-g'yoe gheen-koe)	第一勧業銀行 だいいちかんぎょうぎんこう
Daiwa Bank DAIWA GINKO (Die-wah gheen-koe)	大和銀行 だいわぎんこう
Fuji Bank FUJI GINKO (Fuu-jee gheen-koe)	富士銀行 ふじぎんこう
Kyowa Bank KYOWA GINKO (K'yoe-wah gheen-koe)	協和銀行 きょうわぎんこう
Mitsubishi Bank MITSUBISHI GINKO (Meet-sue-bee-she gheen-koe)	三菱銀行 みつびしぎんこう

Mitsui Bank MITSUI GINKO (Meet-sue-ee gheen-koe)	三井銀行 みついぎんこう
Sanwa Bank SANWA GINKO (Sahn-wah gheen-koe)	三和銀行 さんわぎんこう
Sumitomo Bank SUMITOMO GINKO (Sue-me-toe-moe gheen-koe	住友銀行 すみともぎんこう
Taiyo Kobe Bank TAIYO KOBE BANK (Tie-yo-koe-bay gheen-koe)	太陽神戸銀行 たいようこうべぎんこう
Tokyo Bank TOKYO GINKO (Toe-k'yoe gheen-koe)	東京銀行 とうきょうぎんこう

city names

Aomori (Ah-oh-moe-ree)	青　　森 あおもり
Atami (Ah-tah-me)	熱　　海 あたみ
Beppu (Bape-puu)	別　　府 べっぷ
Fukuoka/ **Hakata** (Fuu-kuu-oh-kah/ Hah-kah-tah)	福岡/博多 ふくおか／はかた
Hakodate (Hah-koe-dah-tay)	函　　館 はこだて

Hakone (Hah-koe-nay)	箱　　　根 はこね
Hiroshima (He-roe-she-mah)	広　　　島 ひろしま
Kagoshima (Kah-go-she-mah)	鹿　児　島 かごしま
Kamakura (Kah-mah-kuu-rah)	鎌　　　倉 かまくら
Kanazawa (Kah-nah zah-wah)	金　　　沢 かなざわ

Karuizawa (Kah-rue-e-zah-wah)	軽 井 沢 かるいざわ
Kobe (Koe-bay)	神　　戸 こうべ
Kumamoto (Kuu-mah-moe-toe)	熊　　本 くまもと
Kyoto (K′yoe-toe)	京　　都 きょうと
Miyazaki (Me-yah-zah-key)	宮　　崎 みやざき

Muroran (Muu-roe-rahn)	室 蘭 むろらん
Nagano Nah-gah-no)	長 野 ながの
Nagasaki (Nah-gah-sah-key)	長 崎 ながさき
Nagoya (Nah-go-yah)	名 古 屋 なごや
Naha (Nah-hah)	那 覇 なは

Nara (Nah-rah)	奈 良 なら
Nikko (Neek-koe)	日 光 にっこう
Oita (Oh-ee-tah)	大 分 おおいた
Okayama (Oh-kah-yah-mah)	岡 山 おかやま
Osaka (Oh-sah-kah)	大 阪 おおさか

Sapporo (Sop-poe-roe)	札　　幌 さっぽろ
Sendai (Sen-die)	仙　　台 せんだい
Takamatsu (Tah-kah-maht-sue)	高　　松 たかまつ
Tokyo (Toe-k'yoe)	東　　京 とうきょう
Yokohama (Yoe-koe-hah-mah)	横　　浜 よこはま

hotel, inn signs

Bathroom YOKUSHITSU (Yoe-kuu-sheet-sue)	浴　　室 よくしつ
Bell Boy BERU BOI (Bay-rue boe-ee)	ベルボーイ べるぼーい
Cashier KAIKEI GAKARI (Kie-kay-e gah-kah-ree)	会　計　係 かいけいがかり
Check-In Time TOCHAKU JIKAN (Toe-chah-kuu jee-kahn)	到着時間 とうちゃくじかん
Check-Out Time SHUPPATSU JIKAN (Shupe-pot-sue jee-kahn)	出発時間 しゅっぱつじかん

Cloakroom KUROKU (Kuu-roe-kuu)	クローク くろーく
Dining Room SHOKUDO (Show-kuu-doe)	食　　堂 しょくどう
Double DABURU (Dah-buu-rue)	ダ　ブ　ル だぶる
Elevator EREBETA (Eh ray bay-tah)	エレベーター えれべーたー
First Floor IKKAI (Eek-kie)	一　　階 いっかい

Front Desk FURONTO (Fuu-rone-toe)	フロント ふろんと
Hotel HOTERU (Hoe-tay-rue)	ホテル ほてる
Hotspring Spa Hotel ONSEN (Own-sen)	温　　泉 おんせん
Information ANNAI GAKARI (Ahn-nie gah-kah-ree)	案　内　係 あんないがかり
Inn RYOKAN or YADO (Rio-kahn/yah-doe)	旅館／宿 りょかん／やど

Lobby ROBI (Roe-bee)	ロ ビ ー ろびー
Massage MASSAJI (Mahs-sah-jee)	マッサージ まっさーじ
Men's Toilet DANSHI YO (Dahn-she yoe)	男 子 用 だんしよう
Men's Toilet OTOKO (Oh-toe-koe)	男 おとこ
Motel MOTERU (Moe-tay-rue)	モーテル もーてる

Reservation YOYAKU (Yoe-yah-kuu)	予　　約 よやく
Second Floor NIKAI (Nee-kie)	２　　階 にかい
Shower SHAWA (Shah-wah)	シャワー しゃわー
Single SHINGURU (Sheen-guu-rue)	シングル しんぐる
Telephone DENWA (Dane-wah)	電　　話 でんわ

Toilet OTEARAI (Oh-tay-ah-rye)	御 手 洗 おてあらい
Tourist Lodge MINSHUKU (Meen-shuu-kuu)	民　　宿 みんしゅく
Twin TSUWIN (T'sue-in)	ツ イ ン ついん
Women's Toilet JOSHI YO (Joe-she yoe)	女 子 用 じょしよう
Women's Toilet ONNA (Own-nah)	女 おんな

miscellaneous signs

A.M. GOZEN (Go-zane)	午 前 ごぜん
Automatic Door JIDO DOA (Jee-doe doe-ah)	自動ドア じどうどあ
Bath FURO (Fuu-roe)	風 呂 ふろ
Bus Stop TEIRYUJO (Tay-ee-r'you-joe)	停 留 所 ていりゅうじょ
Cemetery BOCHI (Boe-chee)	墓 地 ぼち

Church KYOKAI (K'yoe-kie)	教　　会 きょうかい
Close TOJIRU (Toe-jee-rue)	閉 じ る とじる
Cold Water MIZU (Me-zoo)	水 みず
Dentist HAISHA (Hie-shah)	歯 医 者 はいしゃ
DPE Developing/ Printing Enlarging	D. P. E. でぃ ーぴーいー

Drinking Water INRYO SUI (Een-rio sue-ee)	飲 料 水 いんりょうすい
Emergency Exit HIJO GUCHI (He-joe guu-chee)	非 常 口 ひじょうぐち
Entrance IRIGUCHI (Ee-ree-guu-chee)	入　　　口 いりぐち
Exit DEGUCHI (Day-guu-chee)	出　　　口 でぐち
Holiday (Closed) KYUZITSU (Que-zeet-sue)	休日/閉店 きゅうじつ／へいてん

Hospital BYOIN (B'yoe-een)	病　　院 びょういん
Hot Water YU (You)	湯 ゆ
House for Rent KASHI-IE (Kah-she-ee-aa)	貸　　家 かしや
Information UKETSUKE (Ou-kay-t'sue-kay)	受　　付 うけつけ
In Preparation JUNBI CHU (June-bee chuu)	準 備 中 じゅんびちゅう

Library TOSHOKAN (Toe-show-kahn)	図 書 館 としょかん
Medicine KUSURI (Kuu-sue-ree)	薬 くすり
Men's (Things) DANSHI YO (Dahn-she yoe)	男 子 用 だんしよう
Occupied SHIYO CHU (She-yoe-chuu)	使 用 中 しょうちゅう
Open HIRAKU (He-rah-kuu)	開 く ひらく

Open for Business EIGYO CHU (Aa-ee-g'yoe chuu)	営 業 中 えいぎょうちゅう
Park KOEN (Koe-inn)	公 園 こうえん
Please ring BERU WO OSU (Bay-rue on oh-sue)	ベルを押す べるをおす
P.M. GOGO (Go-go)	午 後 ごご
Police Box KOBAN (Koe-bahn)	交 番 こうばん

Police Station KEISATSU SHO (Kay-ee-sot-sue show)	警 察 署 けいさつしょ
Powder Room (for women) KESHO SHITSU (Kay-show sheet-sue)	化 粧 室 けしょうしつ
Private Owner KOJIN (Koe-jeen)	個　　　人 こじん
Public Bath SENTO or KOSHU YOKUJO (Sen-toe) (Koe shuu yoe-kuu-joe)	銭湯/公衆浴場 せんとう/こうしゅうよくじょう
Reserved YOYAKU-ZUMI (Yoe-yah-kuu- zoo-me	予 約 済 よやくずみ

School GAKKO (Gock-koe)	学　　校 がっこう
Shoe Shine KUTSU MIGAKI (Koot-sue me-gah-key)	靴　磨　き くつみがき
Shrine JINJA (Jeen-jah)	神　　社 じんじゃ
Temple JIIN (Jee-eene)	寺　　院 じいん
Toilet BENJO (Bane-joe)	便　　所 べんじょ

University	大　学
DAIGAKU (Die-gah-kuu)	だいがく
Washroom	御　手　洗
OTEARAI (Oh-tay-ah-rye)	おてあらい
Women's (Things)	女　子　用
JOSHI YO (Joe-she yoe)	じょしよう

Bar BA (Bah)	バ ー ばー
Cabaret KYABARE (Kee-yah-bah-ray)	キャバレー きゃばれー
Coffee Shop KISSATEN (Key-sah-tane)	喫 茶 店 きっさてん
Dance Hall DANSU HORU (Dahn-sue Hoe-rue)	ダンスホール だんすほーる
Mahjong Club MAJAN (Mah-jahn)	麻 雀 まーじゃん

Night Club NAITO KURABU (Nie-toe kuu-rah-buu)	ナイトクラブ **ないとくらぶ**
Pinball Game PACHINKO (Pah-cheen-koe)	パチンコ **ぱちんこ**
Saloon SARON (Sah-rone)	サ　ロ　ン **さろん**
Sauna Bath SAUNA BURO (Sah-uu-nah buu-roe)	サウナ風呂 **さうなぶろ**
Turkish Bath TORUKO BURO (Toe-rue-koe buu-roe)	トルコ風呂 **とるこぶろ**

osaka districts

Dojima (Doe-jee-mah)	堂　　島 どうじま
Dotonbori (Doe-tone-boe-ree)	道　頓　堀 どうとんぼり
Itami (Airport) (Ee-tah-me)	伊　　丹 いたみ
Midosuji (Me-doe-sue-jee)	御　堂　筋 みどうすじ
Nakanoshima (Nah-kah-noe- she-mah)	中　之　島 なかのしま

Nanba (Nahn-bah)	難　　波 なんば
Sen-nichimae (Sane-nee-chee my)	千　日　前 せんにちまえ
Shin Osaka (Sheen oh-sah-kah)	新　大　阪 しんおおさか
Shinsaibashi (Sheen-sie-bah-she)	心　斎　橋 しんさいばし
Umeda (Uu-may-dah)	梅　　田 うめだ

post office signs

Address ATENA (Ah-tay-nah)	宛　　名 あてな
Air Mail KOKU BIN (Koe-kuu been)	航　空　便 こうくうびん
Envelopes FUTO (Fuu-toe)	封　　筒 ふうとう
Express SOKUTATSU (Soe-kuu-tot-sue)	速　　達 そくたつ
Mail YUBIN (You-been)	郵　　便 ゆうびん

Mail Box YUBIN POSUTO (You-bean poe-sue-toe)	郵便ポスト ゆうびんぽすと
Metro Tokyo District TONAI (Toe-nie)	都　　内 とない
Money Order KAWASE (Kah-wah-say)	為　　替 かわせ
Other than Tokyo CHIHO (Chee-Hoe)	地　　方 ちほう
Parcels KOZUTSUMI (Koe-zoot-sue-me)	小　　包 こづつみ

Postcard HAGAKI (Ha-gah-key)	は が き
Post office YUBIN KYOKU (You-bean k'yoe-kuu)	郵 便 局 ゆうびんきょく
Registered Mail KAKITOME (Kah-key-toe-may)	書 留 かきとめ
Sea Mail FUNA BIN (Fuu-nah been)	船 便 ふなびん
Stamps KIITE (Keet-tay)	切 手 きって

restaurant signs

Cashier KAIKEI or REJI (Kie-kay-e/Ray-jee)	会計／レジ かいけい／れじ
Chinese Food CHUKA RYORI (Chuu-kah rio-ree)	中華料理 ちゅうかりょうり
European Food SEIYO RYORI (Say-e-yoe rio-ree)	西洋料理 せいようりょうり
Japanese Food NIHON RYORI (Nee-hone rio-ree)	日本料理 にほんりょうり
Menu MENYU (Mane-n'you)	メニュー めにゅー

Noodles MEN (Mane)	めん
Oden ODEN (Oh-dane)	おでん
Restaurant RESUTORAN (Rays-toe-rahn)	レストラン れすとらん
Shabu Shabu SHABU SHABU (Shah-buu shah-buu)	しゃぶしゃぶ
Shokudo Restaurant SHOKUDO (Show-kuu-doe)	食堂 しょくどう

Soba Restaurant SOBA YA (Soe-bah yah)	そ ば や
Sushi Restaurant SUSHI YA (Süe-she yah)	す し や
Tempura Restaurant TEMPURA YA (Tame-puu-rah yah)	てんぷらや
Yakitori Restaurant YAKITORI YA (Yah-key-toe-ree yah)	焼 鳥 や やきとりや
Whale Meat Restaurant KUJIRA YA (Kuu-jee-rah rah)	くじらや

shopping signs

Barber Shop REHATSU TEN (Ree-hot-sue tane)	理 髪 店 りはつてん
Beauty Parlor BIYO SHITSU (Bee-yoe sheet-sue)	美 容 室 びようしつ
Book Shop HON YA (Hone yah)	本　　　屋 ほんや
Bread Shop PAN YA (Pahn yah)	パ ン 屋 ぱんや
Department Store DEPATO or HYAKKA TEN (Day-pah-toe) (He-yahk-kah tane)	デパート/百貨店 でぱーと／ひゃっかてん

Drug Store YAKKYOKU (Yahk-k'yoe-kuu)	薬　　　局 やっきょく
Folkcraft MINGEIHIN (Mean-gay-e-heen)	民　芸　品 みんげいひん
Jewelry Shop HOSEKI TEN (Hoe-say-key tane)	宝　石　店 ほうせきてん
Meat Shop NIKU YA (Nee-kuu yah)	肉　　　屋 にくや
No Smoking KIN-EN (Keen-inn)	禁　　　煙 きんえん

Sale SERU or TOKUBAI (Say-rue/Toe-kuu-by)	セール／特売 せーる／とくばい
Shop MISE (Me-say)	店 みせ
Smoking Area KITSUEN JO (Keet-sue-inn joe)	喫 煙 所 きつえんじょ
Sold Out URIKIRE (Ou-ree-key-ray)	売 切 れ うりきれ
Watch Shop TOKEI YA (Toe-kay-e yah)	時 計 屋 とけいや

DEPARTMENT STORES

Daimaru (Die-mah-rue)	大　　丸 だいまる
Hankyu (Hahn-que)	阪　　急 はんきゅう
Isetan (Ee-say-tahn)	伊　勢　丹 いせたん
Keio (Kay-e-oh)	京　　王 けいおう
Matsuya (Mot-sue-yah)	松　　屋 まつや

Matsuzakaya (Mot-sue-zah-kah-yah)	松　坂　屋 まつざかや
Mitsukoshi (Meet-sue-koe-she)	三　　越 みつこし
Odakyu (Oh-dah-que)	小　田　急 おだきゅう
Seibu (Say-bue)	西　　武 せいぶ
Sogo (Soe-go)	そ　ご　う

Takashimaya (Tah-kah-she-mah-yah)	高 島 屋 たかしまや
Tokyu (Toe-que)	東　　　急 とうきゅう

subway signs

Chiyoda Line CHIYODA SEN (Chee-yoe-dah sen)	千代田線 ちよだせん
Ginza Line GINZA SEN (Geen-zah sen)	銀 座 線 ぎんざせん
Hibiya Line HIBIYA SEN (He bee-yah sen)	日比谷線 ひびやせん
Marunouchi Line MARUNOUCHI SEN (Mah-rue-no-uu choe sen)	丸ノ内線 まるのうちせん
Toei-ichigo Line TOEI-ICHIGO SEN (Toe-aa-ee- ee chee-go sen)	都営1号線 とえいいちごうせん

Toei-Rokugo Line TOEI-ROKUGO SEN (Toe-aa-ee-roe kuu-go sen)	都営6号線 とえいろくごうせん
Tozai Line TOZAI SEN (Toe-zie sen)	東 西 線 とうざいせん
Yuraku-cho Line YURAKU-CHO SEN (You-rah-kuu-choe sen)	有楽町線 ゆうらくちょうせん
Osaka Subway Lines 大 阪 地下鉄	
Chuo Line CHUO SEN (Chuu-oh sen)	中 央 線 ちゅうおうせん

Midosuji Line MIDOSUJI SEN (Me-doe-sue-jee sen)	御堂筋線 みどうすじせん
Sakaisuji Line SAKAISUJI SEN (Sah-kie-sue-jee sen)	堺 筋 線 さかいすじせん
Sennichimae Line SEN-NICHI MAE SEN (Sane-nee- chee-mah-aa sen)	千日前線 せんにちまえせん
Tanimachi Line TANI-MACHI SEN (Tah-nee-mah-chee sen)	谷 町 線 たにまちせん
Yotsubashi Line YOTSUBASHI SEN (Yot'sue-bah-she sen)	四ツ橋線 よつばしせん

taxi signs

Automatic Door JIDO DOA (Jee-doe doe-ah)	自動ドア じどうどあ
Danger-Do Not Open HIRAKU TO KIKEN (He-rah-kuu toe key-kane)	開くと危険 ひらくときけん
Fare Meter RYOKIN META (Rio-keen maa-tah)	料金メーター りょうきんめーたー
Individual Owner KOJIN (Koe-jeen)	個　　　人 こじん
Late Night Fares YAKAN WARIMASHI RYOKIN (Yah-kahn wah-ree-mah-she rio-keen)	夜間割増料金 やかんわりましりょうきん

Out of Service KAISO (Kie-soe)	回　　送 かいそう
Pull TEMAE NI HIKU (Tay-my- nee he-kuu)	手前に引く てまえにひく
Taxi TAKUSHI (Tah-kuu-she)	タクシー たくしー
Taxi Stand TAKUSHI NORIBA (Tah-kuu-she no-re-bah)	タクシー乗り場 たくしーのりば
Vacant KUSHA (Koo shah)	空　　車 くうしゃ

telephone/telegraph signs

Application Desk MOSHIKOMI UKETSUKE (Moe-shee-koe-me Uu-ka-t'sue-kay)	申込受付 もうしこみうけつけ
Collect Calls RYOKIN AITE-BARAI (Rio-keen aye-tay bah-rye)	料金相手払い りょうきんあいてばらい
Long Distance Calls CHOKYORI DENWA (Choe-k'yoe-ree dane wah)	長距離電話 ちょうきょりでんわ
Ordinary Telegram FUTSU DENPO (Fute-sue dame-poe)	普通電報 ふつうでんぽう
Overseas Calls KOKUSAI DENWA (Koke-sie dane-wah)	国際電話 こくさいでんわ

Public Telephone KOSHU DEN'WA (Koe-shuu dane-wah)	公衆電話 こうしゅうでんわ
Telegram DENPO (Dame-poe)	電　　報 でんぽう
Telegraph Office DENPO KYOKU (Dame-poe k'yoe-kuu)	電　報　局 でんぽうきょく
Telephone DENWA (Dane-wah)	電　　話 でんわ
Urgent Telegram SHIKYU DENPO (She-que dame-poe)	至急電報 しきゅうでんぽう

theater signs

| Admission Fee | 入 場 料 |
| NYUJO RYO
(N'you-joe rio) | にゅうじょうりょう |

| Full House | 満 員 |
| MAN IN
(Mahn inn) | まんいん |

| Movie Theater | 映 画 館 |
| EIGAKAN
(Aa-ee-gah-kahn) | えいがかん |

| Next Week | 来 週 |
| RAISHU
(Rye-shuu) | らいしゅう |

| Reserved Seat | 予 約 席 |
| YOYAKU SEKI
(Yoe-yah-kuu say-key) | よやくせき |

Reserved Ticket YOYAKU KEN (Yoe-yah-kuu ken)	予 約 券 よやくけん
Seat ZASEKI (Zah-say-key)	座 席 ざせき
Standing Room Only TACHIMI SEKI NOMI (Tah-chee-me say-key no-me)	立見席のみ たちみせきのみ
Theater GEKIJO (Gay-key-joe)	劇 場 げきじょう
Waiting Room MACHIAISHITSU (Mah-chee-aye- sheet-sue)	待 合 室 まちあいしつ

tokyo districts and vicinity

Akasaka (Ah-kah-sah-kah)	赤　　坂 あかさか
Akihabara (Ah-key-hah-bah-rah)	秋　葉　原 あきはばら
Aoyama (Ah-oh-yah-mah)	青　　山 あおやま
Asakusa (Ah-sock-sah)	浅　　草 あさくさ
Ginza (Gheen-zah)	銀　　座 ぎんざ

Hamamatsucho (Hah-mah-maht- sue-choe)	浜 松 町 はままつちょう
Haneda **(Air Port)** (Hah-nay-dah)	羽田(空港) はねだ(くうこう)
Harajuku (Hah-rah-juu-kuu)	原 宿 はらじゅく
Hibiya (He-bee-yah)	日 比 谷 ひびや
Ikebukuro (Ee-kay-buu-kuu-roe)	池 袋 いけぶくろ

Jiyugaoka (Jee-you-gah-oh-kah)	自由ヶ丘 じゆうがおか
Kanda (Kahn-dah)	神　　田 かんだ
Kichijoji (Key-chee-joe-jee)	吉　祥　寺 きちじょうじ
Korakuen (Koe-rah-kuu-inn)	後　楽　園 こうらくえん
Kyobashi (K-yoe-bah-she) K'yoe	京　　橋 きょうばし

Marunouchi (Mah-rue-no-uu-chee)	丸ノ内 まるのうち
Meguro (May-goo-roe)	目　　黒 めぐろ
Nakano (Nah-kah-no)	中　　野 なかの
Nihonbashi (Nee-hone-bah-shc)	日　本　橋 にほんばし
Narita (Air port) (Nah-rey-tah)	成田（空港） なりた（くうこう）

Ochanomizu (Oh-chah-no-me-zuu)	御茶ノ水 おちゃのみず
Otsuka (Oat-sue-kah)	大　　塚 おおつか
Roppongi (Rope-pone-ghee)	六　本　木 ろっぽんぎ
Ryogoku (R'yoe-go-kuu)	両　　国 りょうごく
Shinbashi (Sheen-bah-she)	新　　橋 しんばし

Shinagawa	品 川
(She-nah-gah-wah)	しながわ
Shinjuku	新 宿
(Sheen-juu-kuu)	しんじゅく
Ueno	上 野
(Way-no)	うえの
Yotsuya	四 谷
(Yoat-sue-yah)	よつや
Yoyogi	代 々 木
(Yoe-yoe-ghee)	よよぎ

Aoyama Dori (Ah-oh-yah-mah doe-ree)	青山通り あおやまどおり
Asakusa Dori (Ah-sock-sah doe-ree)	浅草通り あさくさどおり
Chuo Dori (Chuu-oh doe-ree)	中央通り ちゅうおうどおり
Dogen Zaka (Doe-gane zah-kah)	道 玄 坂 どうげんざか
Ginza Dori (Gheen-zah doe-ree)	銀座通り ぎんざどおり

Harumi Dori (Hah-rue-me doe-ree)	晴見通り はるみどおり
Hibiya Dori (He-bee-yah doe-ree)	日比谷通り ひびやどおり
Kaigan Dori (Kie-ghan doe-ree)	海岸通り かいがんどおり
Kokusai Dori (Koke-sie doe ree)	国際通り こくさいどおり
Kuramae Dori (Kuu-rah-my doe-ree)	蔵前通り くらまえどおり

Meguro Dori (May-guu-roe doe-ree)	目黒通り めぐろどおり
Meiji Dori (May-ee-jee doe-ree)	明治通り めいじどおり
Mejiro Dori (May-jee-roe doe-ree)	目白通り めじろどおり
Okubo Dori (Oh-kuu-bow doe-ree)	大久保通り おおくぼどおり
Omote Sando (Oh-moe-tay Sahn-doe)	表 参 道 おもてさんどう

Sakurada Dori (Sah-kuu-rah-dah doe-ree)	桜田通り さくらだどおり
Shinjuku Dori (Sheen-juu-kuu doe-ree)	新宿通り しんじゅくどおり
Shin Ohashi Dori (Sheen Oh-hah-she doe-ree)	新大橋通り しんおおはしどおり
Showa Dori (Show-wah doe-ree)	昭和通り しょうわどおり
Sotobori Dori (Soe-toe-boe-ree doe-ree)	外堀通り そとぼりどおり

Uchibori Dori (Uu-chee-bor-ree doe-ree)	内堀通り うちぼりどおり
Waseda Dori (Wah-say-dah doe-ree)	早稲田通り わせだどおり
Yamate Dori (Yah-mah-tay doe-ree)	山手通り やまてどおり
Yasukuni Dori (Yah-sue-kuu-nee doe-ree)	靖国通り やすくにどおり

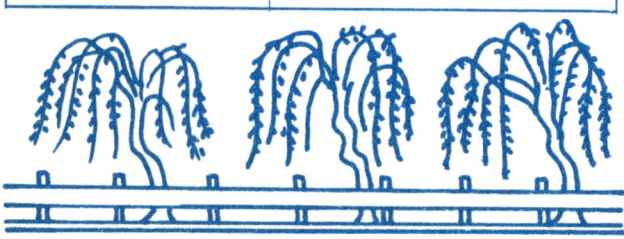

train signs

Accommoda-tion train KAKUEKI TEISHA (Kah-kuu-aa-key tay-shah)	各駅停車 かくえきていしゃ
Boarding Platform NORIBA No-ree-bah)	乗り場 のりば
Central gate CHUO-GUCHI (Chuu-oh guu-chee)	中央口 ちゅうおうぐち
Cloakroom for Hand-baggage TENIMOTSU ICHIJI AZUKARISHO (Tay-nee-mote-sue ah-zoo-kah-ree-show)	手荷物預り所 てにもつあずかりしょ
Destination IKISAKI (Ee-kee sah-key)	行先 いきさき

Dining Car SHOKUDO SHA (Show-kuu-doe- shah)	食 堂 車 しょくどうしゃ
Down (Departing) Exit ORI GUCHI (Oh-ree guu-chee)	降 り 口 おりぐち
East Gate HIGASHI GUCHI (He-gah-she guu-chee)	東　　口 ひがしぐち
Entrance IRI -GUCH (Ee-ree-guu-chee)	入　　口 いりぐち
Exit DE-GUCHI (Day-guu-chee)	出　　口 でぐち

Express KYUKO (Que-koe)	急 行 きゅうこう
Fares UNCHIN (Uun-cheen)	運 賃 うんちん
Green (First) Class GURIIN SHA (gu-reen-shah)	グリーン車 ぐりーんしゃ
Japan National Railway (J.N.R.) KOKUTETSU (Koe-kuu-tate-sue)	国 鉄 こくてつ
Limited Express JUNKYU (June-que)	準 急 じゅんきゅう

Money Changing Machine RYOGAE-KI (Rio-guy-key)	両 替 機 りょうがえき
New Trunk Line SHINKAN SEN (Sheen-kahn sen)	新 幹 線 しんかんせん
North Gate KITA GUCHI (Key-tah guu-chee)	北 口 きたぐち
One-Way Ticket KATAMICHI (Kah-tah-me-chee)	片 道 かたみち
Open Seating JIYU SEKI (Jee-you saa-key)	自 由 席 じゆうせき

Ordinary (Second) Class IPPAN SHA (Eep-pahn-shah)	一 般 車 いっぱんしゃ
Passageway TSURO (T'sue-roe)	通 路 つうろ
Reserved Seat SHITEI SEKI (Shee-tay Saa-key)	指 定 席 していせき
Round-Trip Ticket OFUKU (Oh-fuu-kuu)	往 復 おうふく
Sleeper SHINDAI SHA (Sheen-die shah)	寝 台 車 しんだいしゃ

South Gate MINAMI GUCHI (Me-nah-me guu-chee)	南　　口 みなみぐち
Special Express TOKKYU (Toke-Que)	特　　急 とっきゅう
Special Express Bullet Train KODOMA (Koe-dah-mah)	こ　だ　ま
Super Express Bullet Train HIKARI (He-kah-ree)	ひ　か　り
Station EKI (Aa-key)	駅 えき

Ticket KIPPU (Keep-puu)	切　　符 きっぷ
Ticket Window KIPPU URIBA (Keep-puu uu-ree-bah)	切符売場 きっぷうりば
Ticket Vending Machine KIPPU HANBAI-KI (Kee-puu hahn-bie-key)	(切符)販売機 (きっぷ)はんばいき
Timetable JIKOKU HYO (Jee-koe-kuu h'yoe)	時　刻　表 じこくひょう
Train KISHA (Key-shah)	汽　　車 きしゃ

Transfer NORIKAE (No-ree-kie)	乗 換 え のりかえ
Up (Boarding Entrance) NOBORI GUCHI (No-boe-ree guu-chee)	昇 り 口 のぼりぐち
West Gate NISHI GUCHI (Nee-she guu-chee)	西 口 にしぐち
Wicket KAISAISU GUCHI (Kie-sot-sue guu-chee)	改 札 口 かいさつぐち

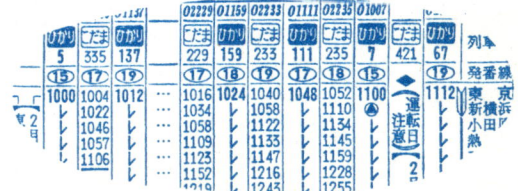

train lines in tokyo

*Chuo Line (Sen) (Chuu-oh sen)	中央線 ちゅうおうせん
Denentoshi Sen (Dane-in-toe-she sen)	田園都市線 でんえんとしせん
Ikebukuro Sen (Ee-kay-buu-kuu-roe Sen)	池袋線 いけぶくろせん
Ikegami Sen (Ee-kay-gah-me sen)	池上線 いけがみせん
Inokashira Sen (Ee-no-kah-she-rah sen)	井ノ頭線 いのかしらせん

* Joban Sen (Joe-bahn sen)	常 磐 線 じょうばんせん
Keihin Kyuko (Kay-heen que-koe) sen	京浜急行 けいひんきゅうこう
* Keihin Tohoku Sen (Kay-heen toe-hoe-kuu sen)	京浜東北線 けいひんとうほくせん
Keio Sen (Kay-ee-oh sen)	京 王 線 けいおうせん
Kokubunji Sen (Koe-kuu-bune-jee sen)	国分寺線 こくぶんじせん

* Kokutetsu Sen (Koe-kuu-tate-sue sen)	国 鉄 線 こくてつせん
Mekama Sen (May-kah-mah sen)	目 蒲 線 めかません
* Musashino Sen (Muu-sah-she-no sen)	武蔵野線 むさしのせん
* Nanbu Sen (Nahn-buu sen)	南 武 線 なんぶせん
Odakyu Dentetsu (Oh-dah-que dane-tate-sue)	小田急電鉄 おだきゅうでんてつ

Non-Marked =Private lines

*Sagami Sen (Sah-gah-me sen)	相 模 線 さがみせん
Shinjuku Sen (Sheen-juu-kuu sen)	新 宿 線 しんじゅくせん
* Sobu Sen (Soe-buu sen)	総 武 線 そうぶせん
Tobu Sen (Toe-buu sen)	東 武 線 とうぶせん
Tojo Sen (Toe-joe sen)	東 上 線 とうじょうせん

*Tokaido Hon sen (Toe-kie-doe hone-sen)	東海道本線 とうかいどうほんせん
Toyoko Sen (Toe-yoe-koe sen)	東　横　線 とうよこせん
*　Yamanote Sen (Yah-mah-no-tay sen)	山　手　線 やまのてせん
*　Yokohama Sen (Yoe-koe-hah-mah sen)	横　浜　線 よこはません
*　Yokosuka Sen (Yoe-koes-kah sen)	横須賀線 よこすかせん

warning signs

Caution/ Careful CHUI (Chuu-ee)	注　　意 ちゅうい
Danger KIKEN (Key-kane)	危　　険 きけん
Don't Cross WATARU NA (Wah-tah-rue Nah)	わたるな
Don't Touch SAWARU NA (Sah-wah-rue Nah)	さわるな
No Admittance TACHI-IRI KINSHI (Tah-chee-ee-ree keen-she)	立入禁止 たちいりきんし

No Photographing SATSUEI KINSHI (Sot-sue-aa-ee keen-she)	撮影禁止 さつえいきんし
No Smoking KIN EN (Keen inn)	禁　　　煙 きんえん
No Swimming SUIEI KINSHI (Sue-ee-aa-ee keen-she)	水泳禁止 すいえいきんし
Quiet SEISHUKU (Say-ee-shuu-kuu)	静　　　粛 せいしゅく
Safety First ANZEN DAIICHI (Ahn-zen die-ee-chee)	安全第一 あんぜんだいいち

traffic signs
Driving/Street-Highway Signs

 **Arrow Direction Only**	指定方向進行 SHITEI-HOKO SHINKO (she-tay- hoe-koe sheen-koe)
 **Center-Line**	中 央 線 CHU-O SEN (chuu-oh sen)
 **Dangerous Curves**	つづら折れ TSUZURA ORE (t'sue-zoo-rah-oh-ray)
 **Detour**	迂　　　　回 (uu-kie)
 **Height Limit**	高さ制限 TAKASA SEIGEN (tah-kah-sah say-gane)

 **Honk Horn**	警笛鳴らせ KEITEKI NARASE (kay-tay-key nah-rah-say)
 **Left Turn Any Time**	左 折 可 SASETSU KA (sah-set′sue kah)
 **Level Railroad Crossing**	踏切あり FUMIKIRI ARI (fuu-me-key-ree ah-ree)
 **No Entry**	進入禁止 SHIN-NYU KINSHI (sheen-n′you keen-she)
 **No Automobiles**	自動車通行止め JIDOSHA TSUKODOME (jee-doe-shah t′sue-koe-doe-may)

 No Parking	# 駐車禁止 CHUSHA KINSHI (chuu-shah keen-she)
 **No Parking or Stopping**	# 駐停車禁止 CHUTEISHA KINSHI (chuu-tay-shah keen-she)
 No Passing	# 追い越し禁止 OIKOSHI KINSHI (oh-ee-koe-she keen-she)
 No U Turn	# 転回禁止 TENKAI KINSHI (ten-kie keen-she)
 **Oncoming Traffic**	# 二方向交通 NI-HOKO KOTSU (nee-hoe-koe koe-t'sue)

 **One-Way Traffic**	# 一方通行 IPPO TSUKO (eep-poe t'sue-koe)
 **Pedestrian Crossing**	# 横断歩道 O-DAN HODO (oh-dahn hoe-doe)
 **Roadwork in Progress**	# 道路工事 DORO KOJI (doe-roe koe-jee)
 **Safety Zone**	# 安全地帯 ANZEN CHITAI (ahn-zen chee-tie)
 **Slow**	# 徐　　　行 JOKO (joe-koe)

**Speed-Maximum Limit (KPH)**	最高速度 SAIKO SOKUDO (sie-koe soe-koo-doe)
**Stop**	一時停止 ICHIJI TEISHI (ee-chee-jee tay-she)
**Traffic Lights Ahead**	信号機あり SHINGO KI ARI (sheen-goe-key ah-ree)
**Weight Limit**	重量制限 JURYO SEIGEN (juu-rio say-ganè)
**Width Limit**	最大幅 SAIDAI HABA (sie-die hah-bah)

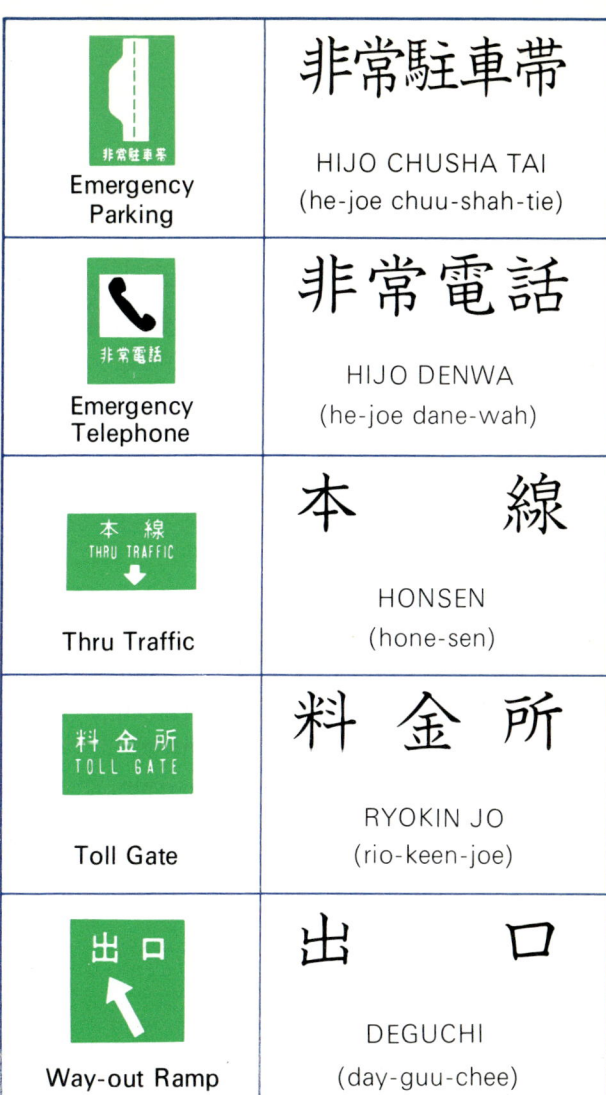

Emergency Parking	非常駐車帯 HIJO CHUSHA TAI (he-joe chuu-shah-tie)
Emergency Telephone	非常電話 HIJO DENWA (he-joe dane-wah)
Thru Traffic	本　　　線 HONSEN (hone-sen)
Toll Gate	料　金　所 RYOKIN JO (rio-keen-joe)
Way-out Ramp	出　　　口 DEGUCHI (day-guu-chee)

Books by Lotus Press Ltd.

NON-FICTION

THE JAPANESE	J. Seward	¥980
MORE ABOUT THE JAPANESE	J. Seward	¥900
THE EMPEROR'S ISLANDS (I)		
—The Story of Japan—	G. Matsumura	¥980
HARA-KIRI HC	J. Seward	¥900
NINJUTSU		
—The art of invisibility—	D. Draeger	¥750
READING YOUR WAY		
AROUND JAPAN	B. DeMente	¥750

FICTION

THE CAVE OF THE CHINESE		
SKELETONS HC	J. Seward	¥1,000
THE DARNED NUISANCES	J. Seward	
	C. Beardsley	¥800
THE DIPLOMAT	J. Seward	¥800
SAMURAI SIX	J. Stanley	¥980

FORTHCOMING FROM LOTUS PRESS

IAI-JUTSU	
—The art of Drawing the Sword—	D. Craig
THE EMPEROR'S ISLANDS (II)	
—The Story of Japan—	G. Matsumura
MAN'S GUIDE TO THE ORIENT	B. DeMente

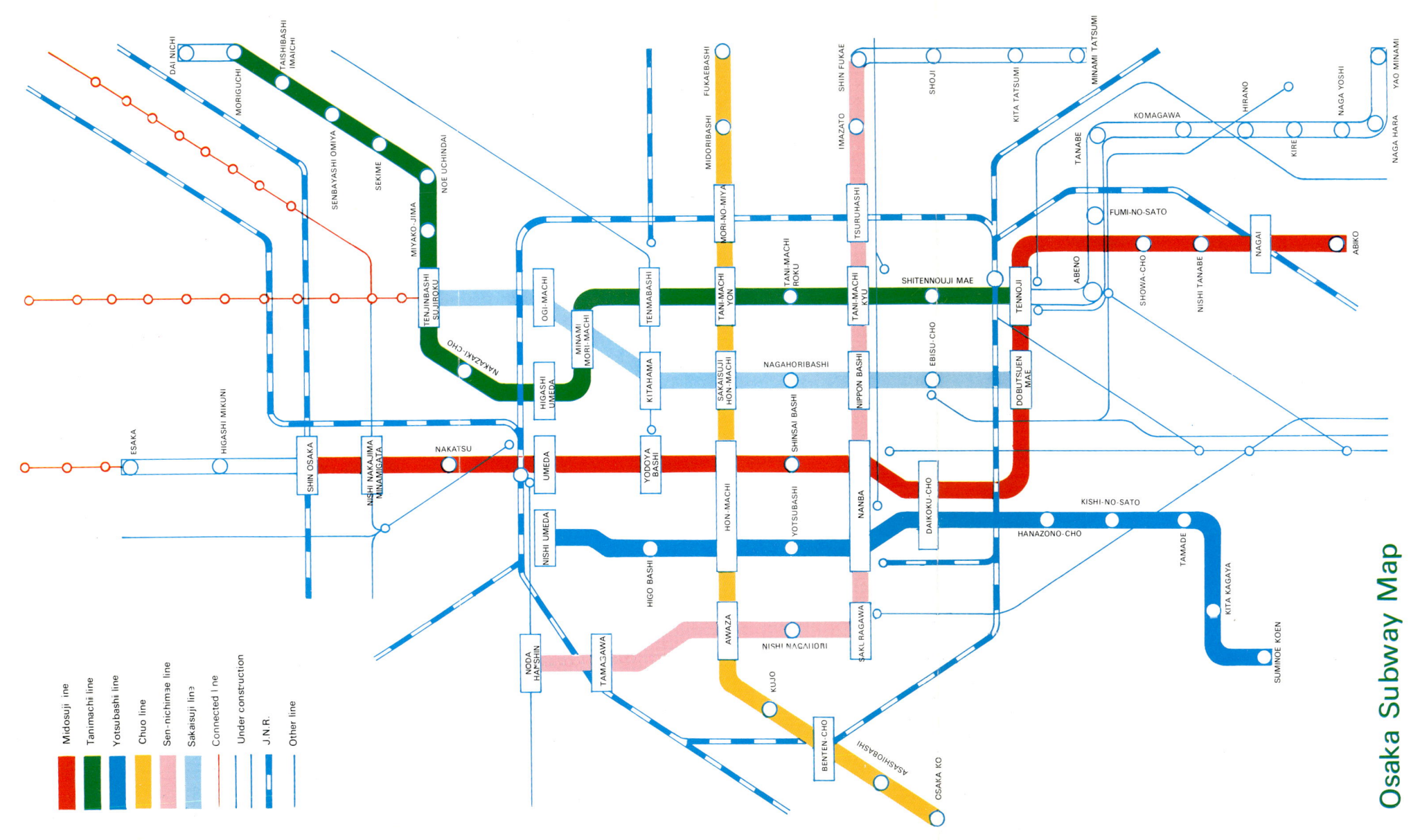

Osaka Subway Map

Midosuji line
Tanimachi line
Yotsubashi line
Chuo line
Sen-nichimae line
Sakaisuji line
Connected line
Under construction
J.N.R.
Other line

Tokyo Subway Map

Legend

- Ginza line
- Marunouchi line
- Hibiya line
- Tozai line
- Chiyoda line
- Yuraku-cho line
- Toei-Ichigo line
- Toei-Rokugo line
- J.N.R.
- Other line
- Inter-change

Stations

NISHI TAKASHIMADAIRA, SHIN TAKASHIMADAIRA, TAKASHIMADAIRA, NISHIDAI, HASUNE, SHIMURA SANCHOME, SHIMURA SAKAUE, MOTO HASUNUMA, ITABASHI HON-CHO, ITABASHI KUYAKUSHO MAE, SHIN ITABASHI, NISHI SUGAMO, SUGAMO, SENGOKU, HAKUSAN, KASUGA, HONGO SANCHOME

KITA KASUKABE, MACHIYA, KITA SENJU, AYASE, ABIKO, AOTO, OSHIAGE, HONJO AZUMABASHI, KURAMAE, ASAKUSA, ASAKUSA-BASHI, HIGASHI NIHONBASHI, NISHI FUNABASHI, TSUDANUMA, BARAKI NAKAYAMA, GYOTOKU, URAYASU, MINAMI SUNA-MACHI, KASAI, TOYO-CHO, KIBA, MONZEN NAKA-CHO

NISHI NIPPORI, MINAMI SENJU, MINOWA, IRIYA, INARI-CHO, TAWARA-MACHI, SENDAGI, NEZU, YUSHIMA, UENO, UENO HIROKOJI, NAKA OKACHI-MACHI, SUEHIRO-CHO, AKIHABARA, KANDA, MITSUKOSHI MAE, KODENMA-CHO, NINGYO-CHO, EDO-BASHI

OCHIAI, TAKATA-NO-BABA, HIGASHI IKEBUKURO, IKEBUKURO, SHIN OTSUKA, MYOGADANI, GOKOKUJI, EDOGAWABASHI, KORAKUEN, WASEDA, KAGURAZAKA, IIDA-BASHI, SUIDO-BASHI, OCHANOMIZU, SHIN OCHANOMIZU, JINBO-CHO, AWAJI-CHO, OTE-MACHI, TOKYO

OGIKUBO, NAKANO, NAKANO SAKAUE, NAKANO SHINBASHI, NAKANO FUJIMI-CHO, MINAMI ASAGAYA, SHIN KOENJI, HIGASHI KOENJI, SHIN NAKANO, HONAN-CHO, MITAKA, SHINJUKU, SHINJUKU SANCHOME, SHINJUKU GYOEN MAE, YOTSUYA SANCHOME, YOTSUYA, ICHIGAYA, KOJI-MACHI, NAGATA-CHO, KUDANSHITA, TAKEBASHI, SAKURADAMON

HARAJUKU, MEIJI-JINGU MAE, OMOTE SANDO, GAIEN MAE, AOYAMA ICCHOME, AKASAKA MITSUKE, KOKKAI GIJIDO MAE, KASUMI-GA-SEKI, HIBIYA, NIJUBASHI MAE, YURAKU-CHO, GINZA ICCHOME, GINZA, KYOBASHI, NIHON-BASHI, KAYABA-CHO, TAKARA-CHO, HACCHOBORI, TSUKIJI, HIGASHI GINZA

YOYOGI KOEN, SHIBUYA, NOGIZAKA, AKASAKA, UCHI SAIWAI-CHO, TORA-NO-MON, ONARIMON, SHIBA-KOEN, DAIMON, SHINBASHI, MITA, HIGASHI NIHONBASHI

HIYOSHI, NAKA MEGURO, EBISU, HIRO O, ROPPONGI, KAMIYA-CHO

NISHI MAGOME, MAGOME, NAKANOBU, TOGOSHI, GOTANDA, TAKANAWADAI, SENGAKUJI, SHINAGAWA